W9-BXT-457

GREECE

by Joanna J. Robinson

Published by The Child's World®
1980 Lookout Drive • Mankato, MN 56003-1705
800-599-READ • www.childsworld.com

Acknowledgments
The Child's World®: Mary Berendes, Publishing Director
Red Line Editorial: Editorial direction
The Design Lab: Design
Amnet: Production

Design Elements: Shutterstock Images; Lefteris Papaulakis/
Shutterstock Images
Photographs ©: Antonis Liokouras/iStock/Thinkstock, cover
(right); Shutterstock Images, cover (left top), cover (left center),
1 (top), 1 (bottom left), 5, 6–7, 17, 18 (left), 18 (right);
Lefteris Papaulakis/Shutterstock Images, cover (left bottom),
1 (bottom right); Remy Musser/Hemera/Thinkstock, 8;
Panos Karapanagiotis/iStockphoto, 10; Sotiris Filippou/
iStockphoto, 11; iStockphoto, 12, 13, 16, 24, 25, 28,
30; Ververidis Vasilis/Shutterstock Images, 14; Fouad A.
Saad/Shutterstock Images, 18 (bottom); Pete Niesen/
Shutterstock Images, 20; Vasiliki Varvaki/iStockphoto, 21,
23; Grigorios Moraitis/iStockphoto, 27; Vita Khorzhevska/
Shutterstock Images, 29

ISBN 9781634070454
LCCN 2014959736

Printed in the United States of America
Mankato, MN
July, 2015
PA02268

ABOUT THE AUTHOR

Joanna J. Robinson is
a creative educational
writer. She has a passion
for providing fun learning
materials for children
of all ages. Robinson
has written educational
content and more than
100 original stories. Trips
to Mexico, Italy, England,
Canada, and Egypt inspire
Robinson to share
her experiences with
young readers.

ONE WORLD · COUNTRIES

TABLE OF CONTENTS

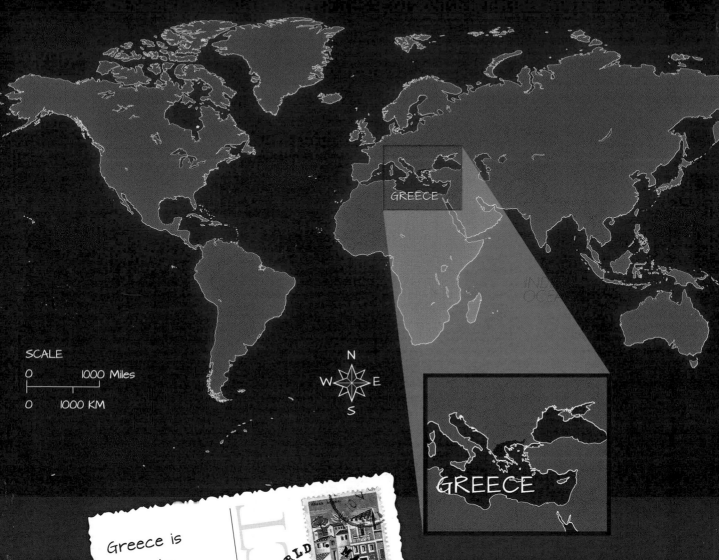

SCALE

0 — 1000 Miles

0 — 1000 KM

GREECE

GREECE

Greece is home to 6,000 kinds of wildflowers. They include rare lilies and pansies.

FUN FACT

ONE WORLD

COUNTRIES

CHAPTER 1

WELCOME TO GREECE!

It is a hot summer day in Greece. To cool off, Greeks head to the beach! They are not the only ones there, though. Travelers from all over the world go to Greece's beaches, too. These beaches are famous for their clean, clear water.

Many of Greece's beaches are along the Sea of Crete. One of the most famous of these is Red Beach. It is located on Santorini Island.

Greece is home to many seaside cities, such as Zakynthos City, which is on the Ionian Sea.

Red Beach has red and black sand. A volcano erupted there thousands of years ago. The eruption left red, sandy pebbles on the beach. Tall, red cliffs line the coast. The water is clear and shallow. There is a **lagoon** in the center of the beach.

The beach is popular with swimmers. The strong waves are good for windsurfing. Some people dive, snorkel, or water ski. People also fish in the coves along the beach. Others enjoy the cafés that are built into the cliffs. This famous beach is just one attraction in the beautiful country of Greece.

Sunbathers relax under umbrellas on Santorini's Red Beach.

THE LAND

Greece's smallest islands are called islets.

Greece is in Europe. On its north, Greece borders Albania, Bulgaria, and Macedonia. Turkey is on Greece's eastern border. Many bodies of water also surround Greece. The Aegean Sea is east of Greece. The Ionian Sea is to the west. The Mediterranean Sea is to the southwest.

Greece's mainland is a **peninsula**. Greece also has more than 6,000 islands. People live on about 227 of them. The rest of the islands are **uninhabited**. Many are very small and do not have running water or electricity.

Crete is Greece's largest island. It also has the largest population of all the islands. Mountains tower over much of Crete. The mountains slope down to plains near the coast. The coast has many natural harbors and beaches.

KEY

12,000+ ft.
9,000-12,000 ft.
7,500-9,000 ft.
6,000-7,500 ft.
4,500-6,000 ft.
3,000-4,500 ft.
1,800-3,000 ft.
1,200-1,800 ft.
600-1,200 ft.
300-600 ft.
150-300 ft.
0-150 ft.

GREECE

BULGARIA

MACEDONIA

ALBANIA

MOUNT OLYMPUS

ATHENS

TURKEY

SANTORINI ISLAND

CRETE

Crete's highest point is Mount Psiloritis.

Macedonia is a region in north central Greece. Mount Olympus is located there. According to legend, it was home to the Greek gods. People consider it a powerful and sacred mountain. The highest peak is Mytikas. It is 9,573 feet (2,918 m) tall.

Greece's land is very active. Earthquakes are common. Volcanoes erupt sometimes, too. A volcano on Santorini Island is still active. Greek homes surround it, and people who live nearby worry about eruptions.

Mount Olympus has high peaks covered with snow.

Greece's weather is temperate. Winters are mild and wet. Summers are hot and dry. Greece has little rainfall. The northern part of the country has freezing winters. Its summers are hot and humid.

Greece is known for its olive groves. Olive trees grow well in Greece's hot, dry climate.

Greece's land has only a few natural resources. They include lead, marble, and salt. Farmers use the land for growing crops. Corn, wheat, cotton, and tobacco grow well. Olives are an important crop, too. They are eaten whole and also turned into olive oil.

Greece has more than 9,000 miles (14,500 km) of coastline. It is the 11th longest coastline in the world.

CHAPTER 3

GOVERNMENT AND CITIES

Voters cast their ballots during a 2014 election in Thessaloniki.

Greece's official name is the Hellenic Republic. Athens is its capital. Greece has 13 regions and one state. Mount Athos is the only state. It has its own leaders and laws.

Greece's citizens elect leaders. This is a part of democracy. Democracy began in Greece thousands of years ago. Today, democracy is used throughout the world. The United States, Canada, and many European countries are democracies.

Modern Greece is still a democracy. Citizens elect government officials to represent them. The chief of state is the president. The president appoints the prime minister. The prime minister leads the government.

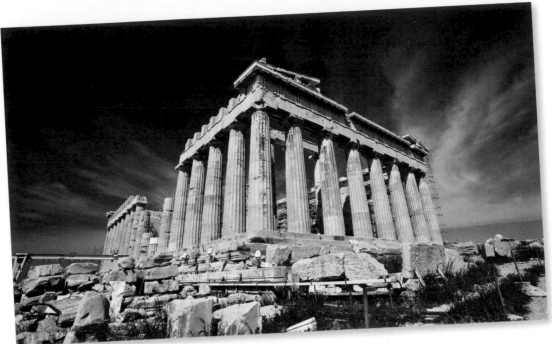
The Greeks began building the Parthenon in 450 BC.

Greece produces many goods. Farmers grow crops. Factories make food, drinks, and soap. They also make textiles, such as thread and yarn. Products are **exported** and sold to other countries. Greece's biggest export partners are Turkey and Italy.

People from other countries like to visit Greece. Tourism is an important part of Greece's **economy**. Each city offers something special. Some people visit the beautiful beaches. Sightseers also explore Greek ruins.

Athens has many ruins. One is the Parthenon. It served as a temple for the Greek goddess Athena. Athens is named

Piraeus is one of the world's busiest ports.

after Athena. The ancient Greeks built the Parthenon on the Acropolis. It is the highest point in Athens.

Piraeus is the main port of Athens. It is the biggest port in Greece and one of the largest ports in Europe. Trade and cruise ships use the port. About 19 million passengers pass through the port each year.

Thessaloniki is Greece's second-largest city. Thessaloniki is known for its traditional market called Modiano. There, vendors sell spices, cheese, fish, deli foods, and coffee. Shoppers can snack at taverns or coffee shops.

Greece's currency

Greece's flag

People have been speaking Greek for 3,400 years. It is the oldest documented language in Europe. When written, Greek uses letters that are part of the Cyrillic alphabet. The shapes of these letters are different than those used in English.

FUN FACT

ONE WORLD · COUNTRIES

A α Alpha al-fa	B β Beta be-ta	Γ γ Gamma ga-ma	Δ δ Delta del-ta
E ε Epsilon ep-si-lon	Z ζ Zeta ze-ta	H η Eta eh-ta	Θ θ Theta te-ta
I ι Iota io-ta	K κ Kappa ka-pa	Λ λ Lambda lam-da	M μ Mu m-yoo
N ν Nu noo	Ξ ξ Xi x-ee	O o Omicron o-mee-c-ron	Π π Pi pa-yee
P ρ Rho row	Σ σ,ς Sigma sig-ma	T τ Tau ta-oo	Y υ Upsilon oo-psi-lon
Φ φ Phi f-ee	X χ Chi kh-ee	Ψ ψ Psi p-see	Ω ω Omega o-me-ga

GLOBAL CONNECTIONS

Many people **immigrate** to Greece. Greece is a way for people to get into Europe. It is central to ports and water entry. Greece is part of the European Union. This is a group of 28 countries in Europe. Once they are Greek citizens, people can move freely between countries in Europe.

Some immigrants come from the Middle East. Syrians and Afghans move to Greece to escape war. Some want a new government. Many immigrants need to find jobs. People hope for a new, better life in Greece.

Some immigrants come from European countries, such as Albania. Albanians make up 60 percent of Greece's immigrants. Albanians move to Greece for many reasons. The Albanian economy is poor. Some people disagree with the government.

Many people immigrate illegally to Greece. In 2010, Greece caught more than 100,000 illegal immigrants. Some people were **deported**. But many people did not leave. Illegal immigration is still a problem.

CHAPTER 4

PEOPLE AND CULTURES

Greece has a rich history and culture. Its history goes back thousands of years. Greeks contributed to the world in many ways. Some ancient Greek inventions and ideas are part of the modern world.

The ancient Greeks invented the Olympic Games. Athletes competed to please the Greek Gods. The Olympics still happen

Men race in the 100-meter dash at the Olympics in Beijing, China. The Olympics have become of celebration of athletes across the world.

Socrates lived in Athens from 470 BC to 399 BC. He encouraged people to ask questions and have long talks.

today. In the modern Olympics, athletes from many countries participate. People watch the games worldwide. Athletes compete to honor their country.

Greece has been home to many respected people. Alexander the Great was a military genius. He was undefeated in battles. Homer was a Greek author who wrote *The Iliad* and *The Odyssey*. These stories about sailors and soldiers are still read today. Plato and Socrates were Greek thinkers. Students still study their ideas.

Modern Greek society is different from ancient Greece. People no longer worship ancient gods and goddesses. Instead, most Greeks practice the Greek Orthodox religion. Most people speak Greek. It is the country's official language.

Festivals have always been popular in Greece. The Festival of Epidaurus is held in ancient and modern theaters. Actors put on plays. Artists perform music, such as opera. Dancers perform ballets.

Greeks celebrate holidays, such as Christmas and New Year's Day. Greece also has national holidays. Independence Day is on March 25. On that day, people remember when Greece became a country. They hold military parades. People carry the flag. They remember fallen soldiers.

Easter is also a special time in Greece. For weeks before Easter, Christian Greeks do not eat meat. They also fly kites. It symbolizes sending away sins and becoming clean. During Easter season, people decorate churches. They hold religious parades. People carry candles, dance, and sing. They eat lamb.

Families fly kites at the beginning of the Easter season on a day called Clean Monday.

23

Modern Greece includes many ancient influences. Ideas from ancient Greece can be seen around the world today. Architecture, literature, and philosophy are a few of the contributions. Celebrations also honor Greek history.

Ancient Greek designs are present in modern buildings around the world. The Greeks created different kinds of decorated columns. They can be seen on the Lincoln Memorial, the White House, and the New York Stock Exchange.

FUN FACT · ONE WORLD COUNTRIES

CHAPTER 5

DAILY LIFE

Greek homes are often painted white so they stay cool during the hot days.

Most Greeks live in cities or along the coast. Greek houses are made of stone, brick, and clay. Doors and windows are painted with bright colors.

Homes are close together. Getting from place to place is easy. In the cities, people walk. At sundown, people follow the tradition of the *volta*. It is a walk at sunset. City residents walk up and down the main streets. Coastal residents walk along the shore.

Greeks can take the subway or a bus in some cities. Some people ride mopeds or bikes. Airplanes and ferries take people between islands.

Soccer is the favorite sport in Greece. Golf has become popular in recent years. Basketball and volleyball are widely played, too. Skiing is popular in Greece's mountains. There are ski resorts across the country. Skilled skiers can take helicopters to the most challenging peaks.

Clothing in Greece is simple but modern. Many Greeks wear clothing similar to that worn in other parts of Europe. Adults wear business suits to work. Children wear jeans and t-shirts.

Many people eat traditional Greek food. Some dishes have a modern twist. Greek food varies by region. On mainland Greece, people eat lamb or goat. They eat pastry pies, including spinach pie and cheese pie.

On the Ionian Islands, people eat spicy food. Dishes often have a spicy tomato sauce. Meals include fish, beef, pork, or

Skiers enjoy fresh snow on Mount Helmos.

chicken. People also eat greens or cabbage. In northern regions, soup and meat are popular. In the mountain regions, people eat goat and chicken. Islanders' diets include fresh, local fish. People all over Greece eat fresh vegetables and fruit. Most meals include homemade wine. Local cheese is popular, too.

Greek desserts are often made with flaky dough called phyllo. *Baklava* includes layers of honey, phyllo, and ground nuts. *Galaktoboureko* is a popular custard-filled pastry. Another dessert is a syrupy sponge cake called *pantespani*. Sesame seed honey bars called *pasteli* are another favorite.

Greece is a country that started many lasting traditions. Its influence has spread across the world.

Stuffed grape leaves include a rice and tomato filling.